Retail

LEVEL 7

/e/

DECODABLES

BY jump!

Teaching Tips

Turquoise Level 7

This book focuses on the grapheme **/e/**.

Before Reading

- Discuss the title. Ask readers what they think the book will be about. Have them support their answer.
- Ask readers to sort the words on page 3. Read the words together. Reinforce that /e/ can have a short /e/ sound or a long /e/ sound.

Read the Book

- Encourage readers to read independently, either aloud or silently to themselves.
- Prompt readers to break down unfamiliar words into units of sound and string the sounds together to form the words. Then, ask them to look for context clues to see if they can figure out what these words mean. Discuss new vocabulary to confirm meaning.
- Urge readers to point out when the focused phonics grapheme appears in the text. Does it have a short /e/ sound or a long /e/ sound?

After Reading

- Ask readers comprehension questions about the book. What kinds of jobs do retail workers do? Has a retail worker ever helped you?
- Encourage readers to think of other words with the /e/ grapheme. On a separate sheet of paper, have them write the words into two columns: one under the short /e/ sound and the other under the long /e/ sound.

This edition is published by arrangement with Booklife Publishing.

5357 Penn Avenue South
Minneapolis, MN 55419
www.jumplibrary.com

Decodables by Jump! are published by Jump! Library.

Library of Congress Cataloging-in-Publication Data is available at www.loc.gov or upon request from the publisher.

ISBN: 979-8-88996-882-5 (hardcover)
ISBN: 979-8-88996-883-2 (paperback)
ISBN: 979-8-88996-884-9 (ebook)

Photo Credits

Images are courtesy of Shutterstock.com. With thanks to Getty Images, Thinkstock Photo and iStockphoto. Cover – Phonlamai Photo. 4–5 – Stokkete, XiXinXing. 6–7 – Jacob Lund, Studio CJ. 8–9 – FTiare, wavebreakmedia. 10–11 – Dmitry Kalinovsky, sirtravelalot. 12–13 – Marc Calleja, FatCamera. 14–15 – stockfour, Hispanolistic. 16 – Shutterstock.

Can you sort these words into two groups? One group has **e** as in **end**. One group has **e** as in **email**.

sequin

vegan

egg

she

Venus

pet

bell

check

Do you ever think about the people who help you when you shop? These are retail workers.

Retail workers do lots of different jobs in a store. They may be involved with restocking, cleaning, and refunding.

In some stores, retail workers might greet you at the door. They may even offer to help you find what you are looking for.

They can point you the right way. They can tell you the exact shelf that you need.

When the products on a shelf run out, the workers will restock them. They check that there are equal amounts of stock on each shelf.

They have to make sure that each thing is up to date and has the right price on it.

Sometimes, retail workers need to deal with problems such as spills and breaks. They help keep the store clean when it is needed.

When people are finished with their shopping, they bring it all to the register. Here, retail workers scan the items and take payment for them.

If a customer brings something back to the store for a refund, a retail worker can help them.

They will check that all the details are correct so that they can repay the person the right amount. The returned items can be resold if there are no problems with them.

Until now, you may not have realized just how much retail workers do.

Next time someone helps you while you are shopping, make sure to thank them.

Say the name of each object below. Is the "e" in each a long /e/ sound or a short /e/ sound?